197

William N. Neff Center
For Teacher Education
Emory & Henry College
Emory, Virginia 24327

WITHDRAW

# BOSS TWEED
## and the Man Who Drew Him
### by Syd Hoff

A Break-of-Day Book
Coward, McCann & Geoghegan
New York

Copyright © 1978 by Syd Hoff
All rights reserved. This book,
or parts thereof, may not be reproduced
in any form without permission in writing
from the publisher. Published simultaneously
in Canada by Longman Canada Limited, Toronto.

**Library of Congress Cataloging in Publication Data**
Hoff, Sydney [date]
   Boss Tweed and the man who drew him.

   (A Break-of-day book)
   SUMMARY: Relates how the artist Thomas Nast brought about the downfall of the crooked Boss Tweed who controlled New York in the mid-nineteenth century.
   1. Nast, Thomas, 1840-1902—Juvenile literature.
2. Tweed, William Marcy, 1823-1878—Portraits, caricatures, etc.—Juvenile literature. 3. American wit and humor, Pictorial—Juvenile literature. [1. Nast, Thomas, 1840-1902. 2. Artists. 3. Tweed, William Marcy, 1823-1878. 4. New York (City)—History] I. Title.
NC1429.N3A5      1978      741'.092'4   [B] [920]   78-5622
ISBN 0-698-30706-2

Printed in the United States of America

Color separations by Harriet Sherman

The Thomas Nast cartoons appearing in this book
have in some cases been slightly adapted
from the originals.

This is the story of two men who made history in American politics just after the Civil War. One of them, William Marcy Tweed, was a very powerful figure in New York City government, who used his power dishonestly to enrich himself and his friends. The other, Thomas Nast, was an artist who realized that with his drawings he could expose Tweed and fight his corrupt politics. When he published his drawings—and helped to drive Tweed from power—it was the foundation of modern American political cartooning.

Long ago in old New York,
one man with a big diamond stickpin
ran the city.

His name was William Marcy Tweed, but everyone called him "Boss."

"Hello, Boss," said the policeman on the corner.

"Hello, Boss," said anyone who wanted a favor.

They called him Boss
because he was the head of Tammany Hall.
That was where greedy men gathered
and plotted to rob the city.

They even called him Boss at City Hall when he went there to visit.

"Here, Boss, take my seat," said the mayor.

He let Tweed put his feet up on the desk
and decide how much money should be spent
for schools, hospitals, bridges,
and other things for the city.
It was never much.

"All the rest of this money is for me and my gang at Tammany Hall,"
laughed Tweed,
and he hauled it away in a big sack.

He didn't care if the streets were dirty.

He didn't care if children had flies in their milk.

All he cared about
was getting bigger and bigger
diamond stickpins for himself.

Some angry citizens held a meeting.
"Let's elect a new mayor
and put a stop to Boss Tweed
and Tammany Hall," they said.

Boss Tweed just laughed when he heard about it.
He hired trainloads of strangers
to ride into New York
and vote the way *he* wanted.

"I can buy anybody I want.
Nobody can stop me," he said.

Boss Tweed's gang at Tammany Hall cheered when he told them
how they could go right on robbing the city.

"For he's a jolly good fellow,"
they sang, far into the night.

One day an artist named Thomas Nast,
who had been away
drawing pictures about the Civil War,
returned to New York.
The moment Nast stepped from his carriage,
he knew there was something wrong.

He saw people living in dingy houses,
and children without a decent place to play.

He saw houses burning
and firemen unable to put out the blaze
with their old, broken-down equipment.

"Who's to blame for all this?" asked Thomas Nast.

"Boss Tweed," people whispered.

"William Marcy Tweed!" said Nast.
"I heard of him when I was a boy.
He was supposed to help the city.
But I guess he only helped himself!"

He went directly to a newspaper office.
"I will rid New York of Boss Tweed
with my pen and ink," Nast promised.

He drew one picture that showed Boss Tweed as a giant thief beyond the reach of the law.

He drew another picture that showed Tweed's whole gang as thieves.

He drew another picture that showed
Tammany Hall as a hungry tiger
feeding on helpless people.

The newspapers rolled off the presses.
People laughed bitterly when they saw
Thomas Nast's drawings
of Boss Tweed and Tammany Hall.

But one man did not laugh—
Boss Tweed himself.
"Nast! Nast!" he said.
"Why can't he draw birds and flowers?
Why does he have to pick on *me*?"
And he tore his newspaper
into a hundred pieces.

Boss Tweed ran from street to street, buying newspapers and tearing them up.

But more and more papers
with Thomas Nast's drawings
were rolling off the presses.
And more and more people
were laughing at them.

One drawing showed Boss Tweed with a bag of money for a head. One drawing showed Boss Tweed waiting to count election votes himself.

Another drawing showed Boss Tweed in a classroom, trying to tell schoolchildren what kind of books they could read.

THE NEW BOARD OF EDUCATION.

"I don't care what the papers *say*!
A lot of people can't read a single word!
But oh, those drawings!
Anybody can understand what *they* mean!"
cried Boss Tweed to his gang at Tammany Hall.
This time there was no cheering or singing.

Boss Tweed went to the newspaper with a lot of money and tried to buy it. "Sorry, we're not for sale," they told him.

Next Tweed went to Thomas Nast and tried to buy *him*.
"Sorry, I'm not for sale either," said the artist.

Finally, because of Thomas Nast's drawings,
the people got together
and voted Tammany Hall out of power.
Nast drew another picture to warn
that the thieves still might try
to swoop down and attack the city again.

In 1871 Boss Tweed was arrested
and brought to trial.
He was found guilty of robbing the city.
"I sentence you to twelve years
behind bars," said the judge.

Boss Tweed went to prison.
"Here's a bigger crook than all of us,"
said the other convicts
when they saw him being led into a cell.

But late one night,
Tweed gave a guard some money
and escaped.

He got on a ship
and sailed far across the ocean.
He finally ended up in sunny Spain.

Here Tweed tried to disguise himself
as a native.
He didn't even wear a diamond stickpin.
But one man thought he looked familiar.
"That's Boss Tweed! I recognize him
from Thomas Nast's drawings in the papers,"
he told the police.

Boss Tweed was taken back to New York
to finish his sentence.
This time he stayed in prison.
He died there, penniless.

Thomas Nast went on drawing for newspapers. He drew a donkey for the Democratic Party and an elephant for the Republican Party.

He loved Christmas
and drew many pictures of Santa Claus.
Soon his idea of how Santa looked
became known to children everywhere.

When Thomas Nast wasn't busy,
he often played games with children
in the city streets.
"You deserve a better world.
That's why I draw," he told them.